Television Made Me The Way I Am

BRENDAN GIUSTI

BRENDAN GIUSTI

Copyright © 2014 Mind Shrapnel

All rights reserved.

ISBN: 0692290648
ISBN-13: 978-0692290644

DEDICATION

This book is dedicated to those who mattered most on my journey through life. Those that relentlessly supported my hopes and dreams. And the ones who brought comfort to my soul as it got battered along the way.

To you: From the bottom of what's left of my heart...
Thank you! No matter where you may have gotten on this ride with me, we've made it this far (surprisingly). Let's see how far we can get.

BRENDAN GIUSTI

CONTENTS

ACKNOWLEDGMENTS

There are quite a few people who helped make this book a reality. Whether it be your direct participation or distant inspiration. Many people have helped shape my life, my mind, my spirit. Many people have helped these words get on to these pages in this book. Directly involved with the tangible efforts to get copies of this book into circulation, however, is a more manageable list of talented folks. Who without the tireless support and sometimes pushing and prodding needed, this book would not be possible.

Candy Blasingame: Thank you for not just critiquing a poem, but also being an inspiration, source of motivation and a true friend. Without your countless hours of work on this book, I wouldn't have anyone to put in this section. So thank you. For all that you've done with this project and all that I'm sure you'll do on future ones as well. If nothing else, you've given me someone to acknowledge in this section. And without that, it would just be a blank page before some pretty damn good poems.

1 SUNDAY AFTERNOON

Prayer

As I attempt to walk in beauty.
Consistently being
      one with the way things should be.
Embracing all that is for what it is.
      For what it wants to be. For what it strives to be.

Lord, I receive your Grace.

As I take a hammer and chisel
      and attempt to *gently* shave off the negative of my life.
Surprised by the shards that surround me.
Stumbling.
      Crawling over.
            Weaving and navigating through the temptation.

Lord, I receive your Grace.

Failing. Succeeding. Trying. And quitting.
Life without end. *Sometimes wishing it would.*
Translated. Copied.
      Reprinted words sometimes the ONLY thread that holds up my soul
when it dangles.

Lord, I receive your grace.

It might all just be the crutch that helps my battered being walk towards a
righteous path.
It might all just be the safety net that keeps my flawed character from completely escaping from holy ways.
Through thick and thin.
      When I'm right and when I've wronged.

Lord, I receive your grace.

3

A Silent Call

Lord, help me see.

I'm on shaky ground by my own accord.

My trembling insecurities. Penchant for the deviants that I, alone, draw near me.

Unable to easily change.
Unwilling to alter.
Comfortable in the painful stammer of deceit.

Wanting.
     My desperate cry of needing.
My soul aching for a new way.
     A freedom I'll only get in God.

My own weakness.
My own instability.
My own flawed soul.

Imperfect *at its core.*

My own doing being the only thing making this unsteady as the Lord's safety walks around me…

Shaky.   *Treacherous at times.*

Unlevel.

My own wobbliness in character, mind, and faith.

Me, alone,
      being the only thing shaking my ability
      to smoothly move from the depths of this man-made hell.

    My own-made hell.

    To the righteous life I know is there.

Lord, I thank you.

      I NEED you.

            Please *show* me.
            Please *HELP* me.

It's possible.
      If I can beat myself at my own game.

Lord, help me see.

"Oh, Lord.
Help me see."

Take As Prescribed

My foul words of hate.
Uttered in a time of frustration.
Directed at you.
Meant, though, in the most general of senses.

My mouth making the sounds.
A symptom of more.
    The verbal cough
    of a bigger illness.
A sickness that strikes down our love.

I lash out and I retreat.
I confront and I avoid.
I stand in front of you.
    In your face.
    In your space.
I demand. And I expect.
I'll disappear.
Become a distant memory.
Leave of void. A hole.
Questions unanswered.

Feelings lingering.
    Left alone until they fizzle into an emptiness.
Creating an aching.
A cold sweating.
A fault-filled fever that needs to break
    for our souls to achieve the goodness they need.
    The righteousness they ought to have.

Cure me.
    Help me.

Holy one, heal me.

I've become stranded by revulsion.
Rejected and forsaken.
Alone with an ugly reflection.
Disliked by my likeness.
The depiction.
        Me seeing ME.
Ailing in isolation.
Ready to revamp.

Recover from the shameful and indecent.

Repent.
        No longer resistant.
        Ashamed of the amoral.

Lord, help me.
        Cure me.
        Save me.

I pray to you.
        Plead for your mercy.

                Rid me of the unfavorable.
                Console me through the adjustment.
                Protect from the maleficence ones.
                As I reject their evil and deceit.

Cure me.
Help Me.
Holy one, heal me.

Lord. Oh, Lord.
Unforced and unfeigned...
Please help me.

Holy one, heal me.

The Revival

Dance.
Dance your insides out.

Stomp.
Shout.
Belt your inner spirit
    up into a sanctified frenzy.

Go on now.
Move
    to your groove.
And
    get happy.

2 MUTE THE COMMERCIALS

Adulation

Why?

A loaded question said with an flippant *pop*.
A punch to the gut that drags out the sound ever so slightly.

whY?

Total disdain.
    Sneering snobbishly
    in this off-kilter fling.

This notion of romance.

    In a time where drunken fucks pass as courtship.

Utter detachment.

    Turning a simple question into a two-syllable
        apathetic story.

        At once mocking her patheticness.

        Equally shouting it into a mirror.

Why?!

Her eyes round and large.
Staring into what she wants to see.
Peering past the truth, into a fantasy.
A reality all the same.

But a lie.

Chin down slightly, head cocked even less.

Nuances of defeat.

Her subconscious projecting what can't be uttered.
What won't be.
Therefore what isn't.

It's a lie. It's the truth. It isn't anything and yet it *just IS*.

Why?

Because *I love you*, she said.

Because I love you.

13

A Look Inside

What doesn't kill you ~~will make you stronger.~~

> *No way man!*

There's not a fat fucking chance that a doped-up junkie will be able to lift any sort of weights from taking a hit of rock, snorting a line of powder, or playing doctor and administering a temporary IV into their feigning veins.

> *No way man!*

What doesn't kill them makes them capable of doing more.
>Needing more.
>And craving more.

What doesn't kill them makes them *fucked up* in the sort of way that leads to others being *fucked up.*

What the fuck are you looking at, they'll ask as they pass a shopper on their way to satisfy mid-high cravings after the sun rose on another day.
>A day starting for some.

A shopper picking up a few groceries before work.
>Looking to whip together the last bit of chow for the office pot luck.

Fucking normal people looking at the fucked-up junkie.

>>Dope-altered minds pondering
>>with the eloquent vulgarity
>>only a user can surmise.

What the fuck is wrong with them, they'll both wonder.

Nodders and fall-outs, calling the overnight fiesta quits too soon.

Chatter and silence, ebbs and flows.
What doesn't kill sometimes slowly maims.
>Simultaneously deteriorating the very thing they are trying to expand.

What doesn't kill you will!

Yeah, people bounce back.
> Those hardships somehow always turn into a sparkly new
> adventure that is that proverbial present we all get after a
> problem - be it nuisance or nightmare.

But fuck!

Maybe the narco-needers got it more right than Nietzsche.

Maybe that trauma diluted our reward and happiness center in our brain so
much that no one is really stronger.
> They're just more tolerant.
> You CAN do with less.

> *But only the man, that moments ago visualized rolling*
> *through life seated in a chair, will feel blessed to stand,*
> *shaky-legged, clutching any railing to take a few wobbly*
> *steps.*

Weaker than the man with him, helping him put one foot in front of
> the next.
But more tolerant to the tragic rarities of simplistic joys he'll forever
> now see.

But like the doper that moved gradually from one bag to two…

> (Or the man who moments ago looked down the
> reality of a life on wheels…)

What doesn't kill you does a lot to you.

It'll take everything you ever had.
    Every ounce of courage to continue.
    And every last drop of untainted, sinister-free, pure good you
        have left in your soul.

It'll take your happiness
    And leave you with permanent disfigurement.
        The ability to outwardly smile.
    Showing the facial signs of happiness and bliss.

        Privately brimming with a misery.
        A demoralized sense of self
        A hope long abandoned.

  It'll take **YOU.**

  ALL of you.

And while it might not kill you.
It'll sure as hell will alter the shit out of you.

Secretly ravaging any possibility of holding tightly on to pieces that
    once were.

Leaving you…

Too exhausted to rebuild what's faded.
Too overwhelmed to live in anything but a haze.
And too devastated to mend the hollows now created.

What doesn't kill you will make you wish it had.

Solitude In The Streets

Want to cure loneliness?
Don't take a stroll on city streets just after the sun has set.

You'll see life.

And despite being in the middle of it all.
    Right in the action.
    Urban vibrancy all around you.
You'll be one deep slit away from the reality of what we've become.

We're all dead.

After all,
    The only difference between a rut and a grave
    Is how deep you've dug.

It isn't anything in particular.
It's the lonely reality that you're not alone.

Building after building.
    Block after block.
        It's happening man.

The faint flicker of prime time.
The pulsating blue-hued lights.
Swelling and popping in an odd rhythm
that's shouting **LIFE**.
as the TV kills another piece of the lonely wanderer outside.

    Alone.
        Abandoned.
           Pacing…

           Strolling.
               Wandering.
                  Searching…

Connected on the inside
   by the stream of lights.
Imprisoned on the outside
   by the disconnect.

Isolated in the abundance of availability.

The whole world at your fingertips.
     Streaming.
         A waterfall of detachment.

Taking a stroll won't cure the loneliness.

No.
  It's an opportunity to reflect on what once was, but is no more.
  See the world as a voyeur.
  Peering through a device to a digital daydream.
  Or catching the subtle flicker of blue.
  Bursting through windows of countess other connected souls.
  Lost in a crowd of nameless, faceless neighbors.
  Knowing that life,
  ever so slowly,
  is morphing
  into a series of
  ones and zeros.

No.
  You want to cure loneliness?

Don't take a stroll on city streets just after the sun has set.

      Participate.   ***Power on.***

        *And **force** another day.*

Dumped

Abandoned and free.
    Rid from their lives as unneeded excess.
    Dead weight.
    The toxic overflow removed.

Ending the ties that bound us together.
    Freeing them from the unwanted.
    Freeing them from me.

But costing me everything.

It was a love that was drenched by conditions.
    Strung together with unobtainable expectations.

I failed them.
I simply wasn't enough.
I succeeded in being me.
    Something beautiful.
    But something just not enough.

Everyone got what they wanted it seems.
    Free of the cumbersome bond and burden of being around me.
    Free from my flaws.
    Freedom.

But freedom has a price.

Not for the lucky ones that achieve it.
    Reaching that state of unending opportunity is paid in full by the people on its other, unwanted end.
    The ones left staring down the barrels of the shotgun of despair.

Abandoned.
    Alone.
The space someone gains with their new found freedom.
    Leaves others just overwhelmed by absolute anguish.

Infinite And Finite

Wallowing in the what-ifs
Wasting away in the when-wills

Dying.

Day after pointless day.
Every waking hour spent obsessing.
   Wishing there was an end.
   Worked up over what was.

Dying.

Walking around. Passing others.
Wishing someone would reach out and zap some form of life into
what has become a decaying emptiness of existence.
   Wishing someone...
   Wishing *anyone*...
      would see past the smile and composure assembled as a daily
      ritual.
But in reality just a costume worn by a corpse.

Dying.

Day by day.
Wasting precious time.
Day by day living in pain.
Day by day existing.
Wishing for something.
Exhausted by the pain of being forgotten.
Too tired to take off the mask that conceals what is.
Day by day. Dying alone. Existing for nothing.

What if...   When will...   Whatever...

Done.

Soda Pop And Discarded Dreams

Remember when we got sodas like losers, she said.

Two losers sipping sodas.
    Watching the wasted wonder.
    Seeing the seekers searching.

A loser then. A loser now.
A soul seeking salvation.
    Redemption of some kind.
    Only to find the church doors locked.

A loser lost again.
    Wondering when God will return from break.

A loser then.
    A loser now.

Not jobless.
Not homeless.
Not helpless.
Somehow just less.
    Not less of a loser.
    Just less.

Left only with a memory.
And a regretful wishing.

A desire to leave this unrecognizable person.
    To return to being a *loser*.
    Sipping a soda..

3 PILOTS, RERUNS AND SEASON PREMIERS

The Old Man, The Stripper And The Girl

Shot out from shooting up.
The old man was shot-skied, bro.
Making laughable rants to the younger generation of dope-heads he led.
Making nonsensical ramblings to the soccer moms he begged.
Looking for that next buck to feed his old, warn-out belly. Long ago
cleaned up from the junk that changed him.
The life he fed into his veins. Vile after blissful vile until it was all gone. He
was no more.
Now the old man was a moving and breathing wad of nothing desirable.
Spending his last dollar tipping an illusion.
A woman moving. A delusion that he was somebody. Showered with fake
affection. Robbed of his money by the sultry, smiling bandit.

The little girl down the road sat by her lemonade stand.
Waiting for a thirsty traveler with a quarter to spare.
Taking a break from hopscotch and barbie dolls to dabble with bucks of
business.
Dreaming of one day.
Planning for someday.
Forever and always living it all.
Learning to be an ambitious lady and slowly becoming a woman.

Fast forward a little bit.

Just getting home was the dancer down the street.
Home was around the corner this week.
Changing daily. Long-term leasing the month.
Motel-living. Sleeping in the transient bed she made.
Twirling around a pole as a penance for all the pricks.
Grinding her way to feed the addiction. Maintaining the only thing that
mattered after dope destroyed her girlhood dreams.
Shooting up. Nodding off. She pumped life into her decaying soul.
Keeping it alive by poisoning what remained.
Taking off her outer layer. Letting strangers touch her inner.
All because the syringe.

Taking a shot to fill the hole. Losing her shot at sterilizing her sorrow-filled soul.

She found it harder and harder to fake a fanciful smile. Medicating more to maintain the fantasy she had to morph into with each passing guy. Doping heavily today to get on an old man. Spluttering partial thoughts of incoherent garbage.

Skip to the end.

The stripper at the motel lived just around the corner from her daughter she couldn't see.

Doing drive-bys to catch a glimpse. Unable to give her any real guidance. She watched from her symbolic couch in her decrepit space.

Desperately wanting to stop. Desperately wanting to hug and squeeze her. Desperately wanting to drop a quarter into her little girl's can and take a swig of lemonade. A swig that somehow would refresh the shredded bond.

She kept driving, though.

Kept driving until she could score. Erase the pain. Injecting life. Forbidden from tainting the life she created. Left to wallow in the remnants of the one she wasted.

She kept driving and the girl kept waiting.

A pitcher full of pink, pulpy lemonade.

An old man rounded the corner and stopped.

Took a look at the familiar looking girl. Dug into his pocket. Pulled out a quarter.

It was all he had left. All that remained after flirting with a fantasy all afternoon in the dark and dingy gentlemen's club that looked at him not as some shot-out loser, but as green. Seeing him for what he could give. He, like everyone else, was green. Just money to the business.

He dropped the quarter. Took a swig from his cup.

Smiled. And wandered off.

The girl smiled after her first sale. Smiled at the fun of working.

Somewhere in between the brain-dead happiness. The smiling, old man, dimwitted from bliss.

Somewhere between that and the smiles of youth. The hope-filled happiness of discovery.

Somewhere the stripper was smiling. Damaged and devastated. Her veins full with the cure to heartbreak. Liquid squirting from the needle into her body. Washing away the desolation. She smiled.

And for a minute, everyone was happy.

But the drugs wore off. The stripper needed a fix.
It got dark outside and the little girl packed up shop and resisted bedtime.
The old man kept wandering. Broke. Thirsty. And friendless.

A Man Walks Into A Bar

He sat on the stool at the bar like a half-dozen other souls that night.
Scanning the menu for a meal he'd enjoy.
He had his phone out next to him.
Headphones plugged in.
Play-list selected.
He was ready.
He was prepared for the night.
To get lost in himself.
Tuning out the world around him as he plugged in and delighted his ears with the familiar.
Eating as he would at home.
But it was his night out.
That looks great, the bartender said.
I think I may order the same thing later myself.
It is, the man said back.
It continued for another 30 minutes.
This back and forth.
Two strangers finding common ground.
I had fun, the man said.
Stretching out his arm to shake the bartender's hand.
I hope to see you soon, the bartender said.

    and they parted.
    each thinking about the unexpected night they'd just had.
    each thinking about when it will happen again.
    when the two can reunite.
    with the safe divider between them that prevents any deep connection.
    it fuels instant intimacy and enjoyment.
    a bar is interesting like that.
    it delights

For the first time, he meant it.
And with that, the two parted.
Each thinking what an enjoyable encounter it had been.
The bartender wiped the crumbs away.
The door to the restaurant opens and a couple walks in.
They sit down at the bar and glance through the menu.

It began all over again.
The glue that builds a community growing tighter with each passing patron.
Lives getting a bit happier.
A man walked into the bar.
We're closed, the bartender said.
Wondering if he'd missed out on making a new friend because the work day was over.
The bar is an interesting divider that creates instant bonds but prevents any deep connections from forming.
It delights.

The Confessional

"Where do I begin," he said.

The Priest exhaled a slightly audible sigh. He had heard all about the man seated before him. And he somehow found himself at odds with the innocence of the man before him and the debauchery he was about to confess. *He brought dishonor to his family. They were ashamed of the degrading, perverted life he led. It was a filthy, vile and destructive life by most outside accounts. Saturated by sex, drugs and Rock & Roll.* The man perplexed the priest, who knew sin might be a stretch. Might not apply to the man. After all, he never acted demonic. Never nasty or sinister. Just the opposite. He was thoughtful and compassionate. He was someone who would be loved by all if he didn't prefer the perverse.

And the priest's job was to listen. You see, words are an interesting thing. And the priest's job was to hear them. And the man knew it.

Words are interesting because words aren't like anything else. Words are powerful. Words defy. Now, it's said that every journey begins with the first step. And while that may be true for storytelling, the first words can also end the whole thing before you have a chance to take step two. Words can cause listeners to tune out. Cause doors to slam in the faces of those unlucky enough to be the messengers of unwanted messages. Speakers of words that end up standing face to face with a wood barrier. Hastily erected to block out the unwanted words. Slammed shut to reject the unwanted syllables strung together in undesirable succession.

You see, words can destroy relationships. Words can end something big before it even begins. Now the man was hesitant with his words. He had seen them insult and offend before. But the priest's job was to listen. And the man knew that.

And so the priest listened as the man spoke.

"Let me tell you about the first time I picked up a hooker," he said.

And so it began.

It Was A Bad Day

The old lady stood in line at the grocery store checkout aisle.
    Aisle number seven.
She gracefully took each item from her full cart.
    Stacking them in an orderly fashion on the movable belt.
    Ordered in such a way that only 76 years of practice can achieve.

        Boxes containing rice.
        Others containing noodles.
        Bags - each with a single piece of fruit.
        One vegetable in each of the others.
        Two cans of tomato sauce.
        One container of vanilla ice cream.
        A two-liter bottle of root beer.
        Orange juice.
        Granola.
        Four peach yogurts.

Those were her favorite.

Offsetting the symmetry of produce and staples was a small bottle of thyme.
It was something new for the old lady.
    An ingredient in a recipe she would try for the first time on Thursday this week.
    Something she discovered and delicately clipped from the pages of the morning newspaper two weeks ago.
    Trimmed neatly from the pages that she read almost religiously each morning.
    Not yet filed away with the others.
        But tucked gently in the left pocket of her collection of directions for meals she now had to eat alone.

It's too bad he isn't here to try this with me, she thought as she stood in front of the cashier.
    Flipping through her coupons.
    Looking for the one that would save her 40¢ more on what she was buying.
    Searching.
    Looking.
    The old lady finding it as the cashier scanned the bottle of thyme.
    The last item now ready to be bagged.

It'd been more than a year.

    But the wounds of her love departing were ripped open and made
fresh with each purchase of something new.

    Each new meal she now created for only herself in the kitchen at
dinner time.

She wasn't sure if ten years would be enough time to erase the pain of los-
ing her husband.

    Her love.

    Her other half.

Thyme reminded her of just how painful it is to do something alone.

    Something that for 53 years was ritualistically done with another by her
side.

    53 years together.

    53 years with the same man.

    53 years as one.

Thyme.

How appropriately named, she thought.

She remembered the time she burned the casserole and had to fix
    sandwiches for the kids to eat for supper that night.

More than the charred mixtures of foods left too long in the oven, she
    remembered two lovers lost in each other.

One serenading the other on a newly-purchased guitar he so proudly
    played for her.

He just that very afternoon learned every chord to their wedding song.

    Strumming it for her while she prepared dinner.

She remembered standing in the kitchen.

    Oblivious to the smoldering pot that could have been the night's meal.

    Succumbed to the overwhelming feelings of completeness this man
    brought to her life.

She felt love as he strummed her a song on the guitar.

    The very instrument she clutched onto after his passing.

        A futile attempt to hold on to him.

    The very guitar she finally agreed to sell.

        Giving in to family pressure.

        Attempts by her grown children to get her to rid her home of
        painful reminders.

Moving forward.

Moving on.

He probably wouldn't have liked it anyway, she thought.

She looked at the cashier dropping the bottle of thyme into the bag, alongside the other groceries.

Trying to comfort herself.

Holding back tears forming as she wrote the check.

Swallowing away the painful lump that formed in her throat.

Realizing again just how much she missed him.

Wondering how many times she would have to justify it in her mind to ease the aching in her heart.

He probably wouldn't have liked it anyway.

It was a great deal, he argued.

It didn't matter though.

It ended up being a deal breaker.

She was mad.

And he couldn't understand why.

And that's why it ended.

The young couple had just moved into an apartment together last week.

Dating for nearly 2 years, they decided to test the waters before tying the knot.

And today was their last.

They were done.

She wanted to be happy.

And so did he.

For a while they were.

Both making the other brim with joy.

But today was their last.

She didn't know it when she got mad at first.

He didn't know it when they began to argue.

But they both felt something was different.

He had a feeling so strong and deep that his gut ached.

Sincerely brimming with pain.

Wondering if they would grow old together.

Something both of them at one time so desperately wanted.
He came home earlier that night carrying a brand new guitar.
   Walking in the house almost giddy with excitement.
   Eager to serenade.
   Hoping to repair by strumming their problems away.
   Making their troubles vanish by plucking strings.
   Singing to her.
   Keeping her.
   Serenading the love of his life.

I got such a great deal, he said.
   He unlatched the case.
   Pulled out an acoustic guitar.
   Rested it on his thigh.
   Kneeling gracefully in front of her.
Listen, he said.
   Strumming the first few cords of a song that defined them.
   Their song.

But she was mad.

   And what once was,
        for a brief moment,
        for a time when the two were becoming one…
   What once was their song.
   Now was just any song.

You should have asked me first, she said.
   Annoyed with the impulse purchase.
   Bothered with not being included.
   Angered by her other half acting alone.

But he didn't seem to hear her.
   Strumming and singing.
   And each new strum caused her to retreat further from the union they
   were once making.
He didn't want to stop.
   Playing the song that had grown to become theirs.

He performed his last serenade.

The guitar he purchased at a bargain price from the widow down the street
   was the symbol of what she had grown to despise.

Feeling unequal. Craving a greater connection.
He strummed and sang.
Each note plucked building courage to leave.
Each chord strummed drowning out the nervousness she felt about
being alone.

And he strummed away.
Giving her one last song.
Once a symbol of so much.
Now a reminder of what was.

That night she packed her bags and moved away.
Her mother's house now her temporary place of recovery.
A home she could use to rebuild and rebound.
She ventured out to comfort herself.
Buying boxed medicine that was topped with pepperoni and cheese.
Her sudden life changes eased slightly from the comfort found after
baking a frozen pizza for 20 minutes.
Only one customer in front of her in line at the grocery store.
She stared at her frozen pizza.
Something routinely passed over during weekly shopping trips by the
former couple.

She looked at the box.
Holding back the tears forming in her eyes.

He probably wouldn't have liked it anyway, she thought to herself.
Justifying her departure.
Reasoning with herself.
Convincing herself that the slight regret she felt would soon pass.

She stared at the box as it moved towards the cashier.
Sliding atop the conveyer belt at the register.

He probably wouldn't have liked it anyway.

Nobody Knows

Rebecca realized it at almost the same instant as Michael.
Nathan wasn't far behind. Coming to the same realization just moments later.
Kelly followed suit later that evening.
And it dawned on David as he lay in bed. Mind still racing from the busy day he had. A day spent dictating the direction of a division on a company.

It struck him as he lay there. As thoughts tend to do. A nocturnal being, becoming slightly visible in those few critical moments where the choice is made - night after night. Drift off to a deep sleep. Mind filled with dreams. Or stay away thinking. Laying. Thinking. Body covered by a sheet. But the mind exposed to tangent filled thoughts.

That night it dawned on David.

He laid staring at his bedroom ceiling. Finally accepting the truth that caused him to deprive yet another night of 8 hours of dreams.
He wasn't one person, he realized.
There was no man named David.

No. As he lay on his back, flicking the tuck of the bed sheets with his toes. He thought about who he was.

He was someone so important to his wife that he required two names. And so important that she gave him several variations of the hyphenated names he was. Dave-baby. David-babe. Dave-hon.

But she only knew the intimate Dave. The Dave-hon that was her partner for life.
She certainly didn't know the "work" David.
The man who spoke with constant authority. The man who probably crossed the line and ended up bossing the staff he led for 8 hours every day. Some jumping so quickly at his every wish that they were almost rented servants. Though they still were paid and kept the titles of secretary.

And nobody at work knew anything about the David-babe that spoke softer at home. Nobody at work had every seen Dave-hon slouch over the bathroom sink. Dressed in plaid boxers. Black socks resting tightly atop his calves. Brushing his teeth. Prolonging the inevitable buttoning of the collared shirt that morphed him into another man.

And almost every morning. As he made the small transformative journey from home to car. He became yet another man entirely.

Davey-boy was a mid- metamorphosed man that only his strangely friendly, yet distant neighbor knew.

Mornin' ol' Davey-boy, he would shout as he flicked his arm into the air above his shoulder. Sending a single wave-like salute to his permanent acquaintance. Bound together solely by address.

Is there anyone that really knows him? He lay in bed wondering. *Is there anyone to really know?*

And Dave-hon laid thinking about who he was. About if he could ever just be David.

Earlier that day it happened again.

Kelly stood in the kitchen. Six pieces of mail on the counter. One by one being opened and filed. Some saved for later. Others junked right away. But the fifth envelope revealed more than the credit card solicitation is was intended to hold.
The fifth piece of mail Kelly opened caused a questioning that finally led to answers. Answers that Kelly sought for some time.
Just fill out the form, the letter read.
Most of it was pre-filled out, though.
Name. Address. Even the courtesy title.
Ms., they checked.
And Kelly stared at the form and realized that to solicitors… To cold-callers and customer service workers… To anyone that didn't know him. He was a she.
And then Kelly thought.
What about all the people that pass him walking down the street?
Was he the Harvard-educated public defender that chose to help the indigent imprisoned instead of taking one of the lucrative law firm positions he was offered so often after graduating cum-laude? Or was he just a black man walking down the street in an almost entirely white community.

Who was he to strangers. He was a she on paper. What was he to the rest?

That day, Nathan wondered what it meant when people at school started calling him Nate.

He went by Nathan. And only his mother called him Nate. But he knew the kids didn't know him like she did. To her, Nate was her baby. He'd forever be the little boy she cradled and cared for. To the few school kids Nathan ate lunch with, he no longer was Nathan. He was now someone called Nate.

And, like any other teenager, he didn't know himself. And as he jumped back and forth between roles he played each day. He wondered. Would he ever really know himself? Would anyone ever really know who Nathan was? Or now, who Nate it?

Michael had the same thing. He was only called by his full name when his parents were reprimanding the teen. Most of the time he was just Mike. He was just their kid. Slowly growing up. But as the distant family gathered together, he was greeted by Mikey-boy and hey there Michael.

They admired how big he'd grown. And he answered to anything even somewhat resembling his name. And he wondered. Was he just the polite boy they hadn't seen in years? Or was he the over-achiever, quick to volunteer, super-student he hoped his teachers saw him as? Would anyone but his best friends ever know him as the rebellious teenager that dreamed of making movies one day? Or would these random aunts and uncles and cousins and whoevers know some other version of the boy he thought he was?

That morning Rebecca started her crisis. It started when someone at work called her Becky. Just moments before, someone else referred to her as Becca.
But 47 is too old to go by Becky, she thought.
After all, she hadn't gone by that since high school.
Becky was someone different, she told them.
And Becca too.
But what she started to wonder, was were those two really gone?
She played a role at work. Professional and proper.
She started to panic.

Does anyone really know themselves?
Is there anyone to really know?
Is there just one? Or are we all just characters portrayed in scenes called life?
And if no one really knew anyone.
Was there anyone to ever really know?

4 TO BE CONTINUED

Epilogue

Art is...

Not the technical, often regurgitated Webster's words...

But those certain, undeniable elements, sometimes overlooked.

The communal sense of art that binds a culture sometimes is lost in books. Novels not commonly read. Books not discussed in a club.

Poetry almost being the ultimate.

The power. The subtle grace a stanza can deliver to the audience of one, sifting through the pages of a collection.

You see, books are unique that way. They offer a form of storytelling that is individual to each reader.

It's something lost nearly entirely in film and stage performances.

The characters in books are not portrayed by an actor. There is no recognizable cast. No, what books offer is a deep, yet loosely defined visual representation of each character. The exact visual representation left to each unique reader to complete in his mind.

Nuances of language acting as the building blocks. The reader constructing the final image.

Books offer an interactive form of storytelling - done in near isolation. Just the reader and the pages. No packed theater. No lecturer. No applause.

The reader is left alone to ponder and reflect. While some books offer quick, page-turning stories, the very nature of poetry (compressed thought) amps up that individual reflection.

It is a burning flame, sparked almost exclusively in the solitude of a quiet corner of a house. You see, that cup of tea, that cozy chair, and that song pumping through those earbuds is a perfect setting for pouring over pages of poetry. Reflecting on the prose stuffed between two covers.

The following pages are intentionally left blank in the hopes that when the spirit moves you, the reader… by actually taking pen to paper… you might elevate this work of art to the next level. Away from something easily enjoyed alone, into a communal experience through sharing your thoughts, reflections and ideas.

You may even be moved to jot down a few lines of your own poetry, or prose.

In that sense, every copy of this book is a unique work. No two copies are alike. Even if left blank, this book offers endless possibilities.

I've done my part.
The rest is up to you.

Dwell in possibilities!

The End.

The End.

www.ingramcontent.com/pod-product-compliance
Lightning Source LLC
Chambersburg PA
CBHW070501050426
42449CB00012B/3072